A Day in the Life of a...

Doctor

Carol Watson

W

FRANKLIN WATTS

NEW YORK • LONDON • SYDNEY

This is Nicky. She is a doctor.
Nicky starts her day at the surgery
where sick people come to see her.

First Nicky asks
the receptionist,
"How many
patients do
I have today?"
They look through
the list of
appointments
and home visits.

3

The doctor goes to her office and
gets ready to start work.
She turns on her computer which
stores information about the patients.

The first patient arrives to see Nicky.
"Charlotte's got a temperature,"
her mum tells the doctor.

Nicky takes
Charlotte's
temperature
and examines
her throat.

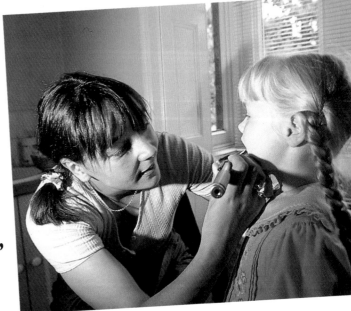

"Can you say 'aah'
for me?" she asks.

"I'm going to listen to your chest now, Charlotte," says Nicky.

"Then I'll have a look in your ears."

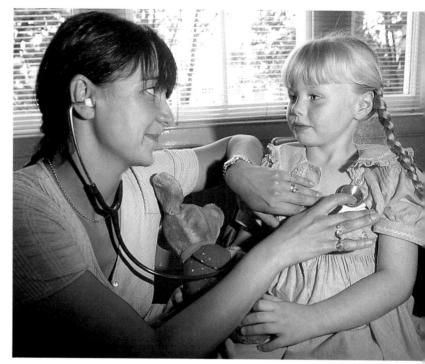

The doctor looks at the computer screen to check her information on Charlotte.

Then she writes a prescription.

"This medicine will help her feel better," says Nicky.

She says goodbye, then writes down what she has done in Charlotte's file.

The next patient, Harriet, is feeling
very dizzy and sick.
Nicky takes her blood pressure
to see if it is normal.

"I think you should go to hospital,"
she tells the patient.
She rings the hospital and writes a letter
for Harriet to take with her.

When the morning
surgery is over,
the doctor reads and
answers her letters.

Then she puts
her bag in the car
ready for
the home visits.

Inside her bag the doctor has
all the things she might need
to help the patients who are
too sick to come to the surgery.

13

Nicky makes her first home visit.
A little boy called Tom has a
bad tummy ache.

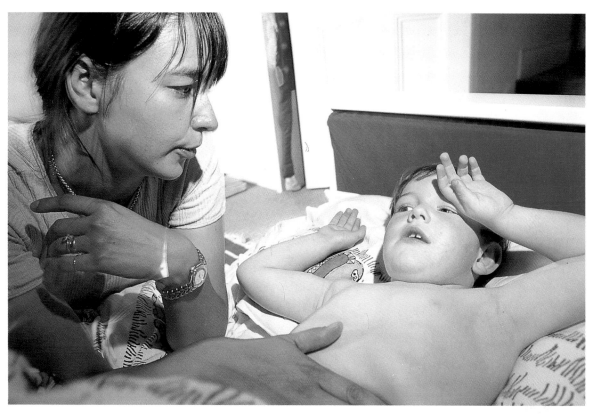

"Where does it hurt?" she asks. Nicky takes Tom's temperature and looks in his mouth and ears. "It's nothing serious," she tells his mum.

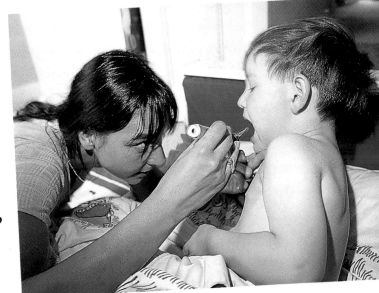

The doctor makes more home visits
and then returns to the surgery
in time for the baby clinic.

She talks to the health visitor who helps with the clinic.

The health visitor weighs the babies.

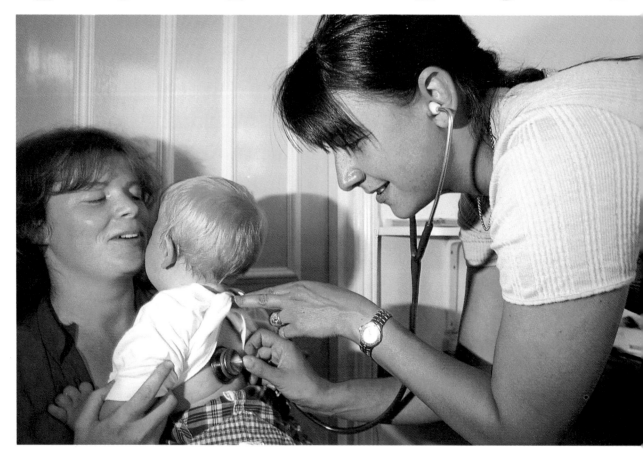

Sarah has brought her
baby for a check up.
"Hello, Ben," says
Nicky.
She examines Ben
all over and listens
to his chest.

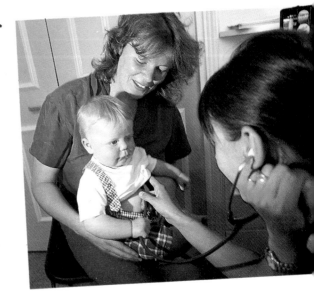

Nicky sees more
babies until
everyone has gone.
The clinic is over.

Now the doctor
can go home.

Make your own First Aid Kit

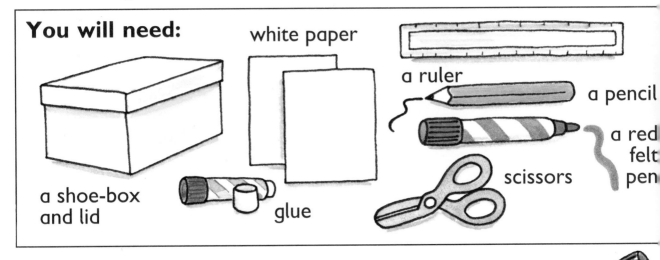

You will need:

white paper

a ruler

a pencil

a red felt pen

scissors

glue

a shoe-box and lid

1. With your pencil and ruler draw a large cross on a piece of paper. Colour it in red with a felt pen.

2. Carefully cut out the cross.

3. Spread a little glue onto the back of your cross and stick it onto the top of the shoe-box lid.

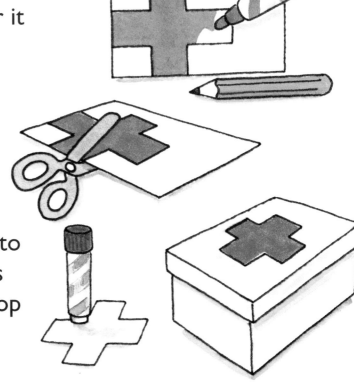

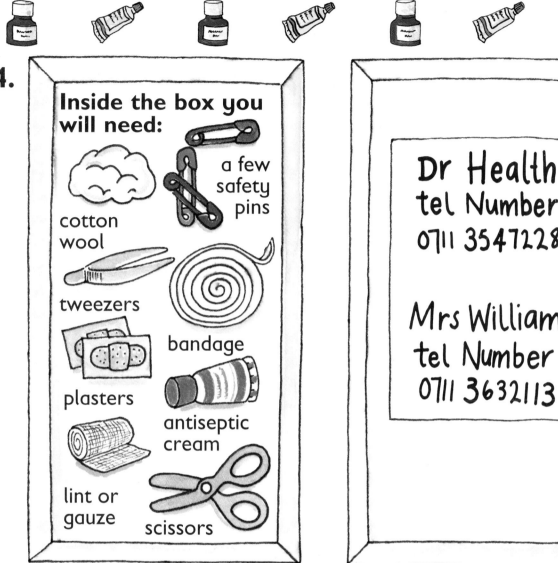

4.

Inside the box you will need:

cotton wool

a few safety pins

tweezers

bandage

plasters

antiseptic cream

lint or gauze

scissors

Dr Health
tel Number
0711 3547228

Mrs Williams
tel Number
0711 3632113

5. Now take another piece of paper. Write the name and telephone number of your doctor and a friend or neighbour.

6. Stick the information inside the lid of your box.

Keep your First Aid Kit safely away from babies and toddlers.

21

How you can help your doctor

1. Always carry a handkerchief. Use it to blow your nose or cover your face if you sneeze.

2. Put your hand over your mouth when you cough.

3. Always wash your hands when you have been to the toilet.

4. Wash cuts and grazes and cover them with a plaster or bandage.

5. Keep away from fires and cookers.

6. Don't touch electric sockets.

In an emergency dial **999** to call an ambulance. Tell the operator your name and address.

Facts about doctors

It takes six years of training to become a doctor. Student doctors study for five years at medical school or a teaching hospital, and then work full-time in a hospital for a year. After that they can choose to specialise either in hospital or in General Practice.

The doctor in this book is called a General Practitioner, or G.P. for short. She works as a family doctor with six other partners and two trainees in a General Practice, caring for 13,000 patients. The doctors take it in turns to be 'on call' (on duty and ready to visit patients at home), so there is always a doctor available 24 hours a day.

Other people that work at a surgery are:

secretaries
receptionists
nurses
health visitors

Index

© 1995 Franklin Watts
This edition 1998

Franklin Watts
96 Leonard Street
London EC2A 4RH

Franklin Watts Australia
14 Mars Road
Lane Cove NSW 2066

UK ISBN: 0 7496 1996 1
Dewey Decimal Classification
Number 610.69
A CIP catalogue record for
this book is available from
the British Library.

Editor: Sarah Ridley
Designer: Nina Kingsbury
Photographer: Chris Honeywell
Illustration pg 20-21: Andrew Crowson

With thanks to Nicky and Tom
Lloyd-Jones and the members
of Seymour House Surgery,
Richmond; Ben Ridley-
Johnson, Carina and Charlotte
Hardy, Carol Ilube and Catherine
Cowen.

Printed in Malaysia